Lifecycle of a Beautiful Woman

by
Ann Weil

photography by
Jillian Mayotte and Kelsey Orr

YELLOW ARROW
PUBLISHING
Baltimore, Maryland, USA

Library of Congress Control Number: 2023934368
ISBN (paperback): 979-8-9850704-6-0

Photography by Jillian Mayotte (jillianmayotte@gmail.com)
and Kelsey Orr (korr234@gmail.com).
Cover & interior design by Yellow Arrow Publishing.
For more information, see yellowarrowpublishing.com.

Contents

For all the beautiful women in my life,
and for my beloved Tony

Acknowledgments

What Next? Anthology, Dempsey & Windle Press, October 2020
"What Were You Thinking, Pandora?"

Eastern Iowa Review, Spring 2021
"Blade Upon Bark"
"On her back her mind wanders"

San Pedro River Review, Fall 2021
"In the Pastel Hour"

Whale Road Review, Summer 2022
"Knowing"

Innisfree Poetry Journal, September 2022
"Life(line)"

Broad River Review, December 2022
"Sonnet While Waiting for the Hurricane"

DMQ Review, Spring 2023
"Into the Folds"

LIFECYCLE OF A BEAUTIFUL WOMAN

What Were You Thinking, Pandora?

I can tell you from personal experience,
there wasn't just one box.

Like the goddess Dolly Parton's
rhinestoned blouse
with its mother-of-pearl buttons
hanging on for dear life,
my closet is full to bursting—
boxes, bags, vases, urns
stacked Tetris-style floor to ceiling.
Trunks, crates, even a David Cassidy lunchbox—
anything remotely resembling a container—
I've got hundreds, each sealed vice-tight
with fishing line, surgery staples or duct tape,
padlocks, superglue, zip ties.
Clearly a lesson here, but . . .
temptation rings the doorbell
and there I am, box cutter in hand.
Yes, I peek. Often.
As any learned scholar or third grader will predict,
an explosion of all the hells thus ensues
and I end up divorced, disowned, or exiled.
Fired, fleeced, flattened, forsaken.
Sailing in a leaky ship sunk by my own stiletto.
Drowning in a misery moat of my own making.

What were you thinking, Ann?

I was thinking, which box next?

Into the Folds

A yellow bird has come
to the window, wings hard at work
but it doesn't hum. Hovers
over the bramble, rests
on a thornless branch.

It is June in Texarkana—heat
ripples from the pavement,
from the chrome on Aunt's T-Bird.
This bird is red, not yellow,
and Mother Mary swings
from the rearview mirror.
Patron saint of sharp curves
coming out of nowhere.
Blue robes hide many sins.

Aunt with the waist-length hair
unpins her graying locks at night,
sits at the vanity. With a silver brush
she ministers—a hundred strokes,
one for each mistake she's made.
Penance should serve a purpose,
she tells me, and tucks a thousand or so
additional blunders and misdeeds
into the folds of her faded blue nightgown.
She crawls into bed, sleeps deep
under the weight of her transgressions.

In the pale morning light,
Mary of the T-Bird unties herself,
weary of the dangle and sway.
The car's crank windows are a challenge,
but she is a woman who knows her strength.
Mary whistles for the yellow bird,
climbs on its back, and they fly away.

Sonnet of Unanswerable Questions

Which came first—the seed or the fruit? How far
east can you travel before you're heading
west? When you forget thoughts, where do they go?

What's the synonym for synonym? Why
aren't buildings called builts? If we're too old to
climb the hill, why are we over the hill?

Are we there yet? What is consciousness? Is
karma real or just a construct? What are
dreams? Why are we here? Is time linear?

Or circular? Multidimensional?
Are we living or dying? Is love all
we really need? When will I be enough?

What is the shape of the sky? What color
is breath? Why do we hurt one another?

The Skirt

Dive bar, snowy New Year's Eve,
my skirt and I where we shouldn't be.

Waitress—Eva—inked and cute
says, "Ooh. I love your skirt."

"Thanks. Me, too," and I do love it, this
silent siren's song, assured lure of men

to its hot pink hugging shores. The neon sign
flashes **OPEN**. I order tequila. Feel its

bittersweet burn, then the full-body shimmy.
I ask the girl for another. "Hell. Let's make it three."

I tease the second shot, suck face with the third.
I'm in a mood. "Resolution?" I ask Eva.

She shrugs, says, "I always fail." Almost midnight,
I grab my coat, but I need to pee, head

for the *Ladies*. The irony isn't lost. Neither am I.
On my way out of the bar, I hand Eva a soft bundle,

neatly folded. "Happy New Year," I say.
A block away, the cold kisses my thighs.

In the Pastel Hour

In the pastel hour between stars and sun,
she backs her neon green Beetle out of the drive

and heads for the highway, another busted up
love affair in her rearview mirror, its promises

fading, falling into that bushel basket of memories,
settling beside an old story in another car,

this time a shiny white Cadillac convertible
with a tiny girl, sobbing,

wedged in the far corner of the backseat,
her big, wonderful, terrible Daddy

at the wheel, tension rising from him
like vapors on a desert road, and he says

*If you don't quit crying, I'm gonna leave you
on a street corner*, and the stillness

quick so quiet came to the car, just like
the silence now in the green Beetle,

where she thinks about the places that hurt, and knows
the truth—if you leave first you can't be left.

Life(line)

Life is you (I mean me) and the new one (baby)
and the other one who comes and goes (husband).

And there is love hanging like fine mist,
a dewy glow on skin. And there is loneliness,

too, in this shrunken world, unpeopled except
for Bob Barker and *The Young and the Restless.*

One day you (I) and the new one (baby)
met another you (Maria) with her own new one (baby),

and the foggy days of hard love that stretched for miles
became brighter, quicker. We (Maria and I) fed

on friendship, raised each other while we raised our babies,
while our husbands talked mowers and mortgages.

Did you (I) mention she was beautiful? Like a sunflower.
Whither thou goest, I will go. But this is not the Book of Ruth.

The first time Maria left me (by then
I had become myself), it was her husband's fault.

A job took them half a country away while I stayed
planted in Michigan's fertile, lonesome soil.

We relied on the umbilical of the phone cord.

The second leaving came after Hannah died.
Maria's baby. I can say her name now.

I don't know where babies, or any of us, go after dying.
And I don't know where Maria went after the dying, in order to live.

15

Knowing

it was a strange place
for a revelation, that boisterous boat
with its mouse ear smokestacks
teeming with hundreds
of laughing, squealing children,
parents bedraggled but happy
to have a cocktail in hand
while their progeny played
with Donald Duck and Cinderella—
still—the knowing came,
as I heard you for the umpteenth time
cuss out Mickey and me, as I saw
yet again your hunched shoulders weighted
as if you wore a concrete backpack
you couldn't unburden
even as our kids beamed and giggled
Look at me, Dad! and I,
miscast as a Disney princess,
coddled and cajoled but made things worse,
the pain unhealable in our home,
on this boat, anywhere—
our love so wrecked
I knew that nothing,
not even a Magic Kingdom,
could save us.

Sonnet for Ex-Husband #1

Some nights when sleep plays hard to get, I reach
for my phone and Google your name, not to
reconnect (no latent love to unleash),
just to see how you turned out, boy I knew

from childhood, whose gentle eyes understood.
You who cradled me as I slept—too much
to drink at the Homecoming Dance—you could
have hurt me. Instead, in my beaded clutch

the next day, I found your note *I love you,
Annie.* You were a sweetness I'd never
tasted. Refuge for the refugee. Too
young, like me, but some ties will not sever.

And I wonder, have you Googled my name?
Maybe not, as I was the one to blame.

Lifecycle of a Beautiful Woman

When time traveling, there is no need to begin at the beginning.

Sixty-one.
I used to be what I no longer am. The switch—no, the electricity—
that lit the room. Powered the whole damn city. Now, I am trying out
that inner beauty hoax, what do I have to lose? Pearl in the oyster,
waiting to be discovered. But to be seen, you must step outside,
and there goes the whole premise. I'm making friends with dimness.

Thirteen.
We've never truly known red, until it pools between our legs.
Against white cotton panties, its special effects are stunning.
First high heels on the red carpet. Paparazzi men call my name.
The light blinds, but I like it.

Twenty-four.
There are 200 billion trillion stars in the sky. We can see 9,096.
I am the one called North.

Sixty-one.
Mirror, mirror, on the wall, who the hell is that? All I need
is a poisoned apple. Ha!

Thirty-seven.
afterglow /ˈaftərˌglō/ noun
Oxford Languages Dictionary: Radiance remaining in the sky
after sunset.
Urban Dictionary: A look of contentment on a person's face
after great sex.

Forty-five.
Silver is the new gray. I am taking the bullet train.

Sixty-one.
Sex remains gorgeous. A Botticelli discovered in the attic.

Fifty-three.
Money doesn't buy happiness, but it can buy a face-lift.
In Pursuit of Beauty has Aging Gracefully in a chokehold.
AG victorious with a TKO (fear of needles).

Sixty-one.
Beginning of the end, power outages. Appreciation. Strength
to turn the mirror to the wall—better yet—fly the "Fuck-it" flag.
Understanding that this body will carry me to the next, each radiant
rendition fading, falling away until the only beauty left is bone.

At the Al-Anon Tables I Learn
to Shut My Beak

My name is Ann, and I'm a junkie.
My *fix* is the fix.

All my birds are arranged just so
perfectly, not a feather mussed,
and should one make a face
or even adjust her perch
in search of comfort, my squawking
starts, then the flapping of my wings
as I frizzle and fuss, unable to trust
that my chicks have their own
methods of flight, that they'll be alright
in a foxed and stormy night, and my constant
ministrations have dire costs
to the entire flock who will not
become what they ought.

And everything goes to shit.

How long must I wait for this difficult truth
to roost in my addled birdbrain?
That it's not my job to paint the sky
a painless shade of blue.

Blade Upon Bark

for my ex-husband

His first knife
His first nick
He hid the bloody
finger behind his back
Snuck past the prophet
at the kitchen sink
and headed for the first aid kit
Just a paper cut he said
Please pass the meatloaf
Seer saw the truth
but held her tongue

Carving boy grew up
but never left the wilderness
Sought treatment and treaties
For years held a truce
taming trees into totems
and birds—so many
ravens and crows flew
from his hands, soared
from the knife, wood
brought to life with each caress
of the blade upon bark
upon flesh and bone
sometimes his own—
in the end his own—

Knife traded for car
Tree feels the impact
Bears his mark

Considering the Vibrator

after Al Zolynas

The idea of it is disturbing at first.
The necessity of a mechanical device
to give pleasure when human touch

is on vacation, working late,
nonexistent, or just not enough.
A jiggling wiggler, a rumbling

thrummer, a distant memory
of the penny horse at Winn Dixie.
I remember finding my parents'

"massager" in the bottom drawer
of their nightstand. It looked
like a hand grenade with straps,

a futuristic wrist corsage
for a robot prom. What prompted me
to plug it in and apply it

to my pubic region, I'll never know.
It's not like I used a blender
or electric pencil sharpener that way.

Ah, but we have always
found truth in unexpected places.
Like the day my three-year-old

discovered "mommy's rocket"
and brought it to the living room
to show Gram and Gramps.

Son, I believe that's a vibrator,
my father clarified, as I died
a slow and inglorious death.

Fact is, there's no greater truth
than a well-delivered orgasm,
never mind its source.

Sonnet for Ex-Husband #2

Early days, you took me to the balloons—
a dozen giants breathing fire at dawn,

rainbow globes in the hazy blue moored by
ropes and dreams unflown. Your camera loved

the morning light—softness captured without
net, gold refusing to be spent, we held

it in our hands. Blessed is what we felt, what
we were, that year and years after until

we frayed. Losing our way was not the plan
yet still we floundered, groped in the night, thought

we could grow without growing apart. Wrong
on all counts, no ease on long haul, the more

we struggled the tighter the trap, 'til one
cut the ropes, let the colors bleed and run.

She Takes a Second Mistress

Brush. Canvas. Pigment. Palette of umber,
ochre, sienna, held thumb to palm by
the woman of words who dared another
blank expanse. Bristle or flat? Filbert or
fan? Choices now make choices later. Still
life? Plein air? Trompe l'oeil or nude? She ponders
shadow, value, hue, imagines herself
with Kahlo, Cassatt, in the sisterhood
of malcontents who stood at easel, not
at stove. She stipples, scumbles, strokes and daubs,
considers composition, light sources,
horizon, stokes the fire of ambition.
She breathes O'Keeffe, sleeps Morisot, and still—
as when she writes—trembles before the white.

Old Town Stroll, Key West

Before the heat, you walk,
shed sleep from tired eyes.
Greet the chickens

crossing the street. Wish
you bent and swayed
as easily as the palms.

'Gonna be a scorcher today
calls the neighbor. *Hotter 'n Hades.*
You wave and sweat on by.

Up ahead along a whitewashed fence
a hawk splays dead
on the sidewalk. She looks

like a Sleeping Beauty
perfect and peaceful and
you wish it were so,

and you wish many things
to be what they aren't.
Cracked eggs to be whole,

secrets to be kept, words
to be unsaid or said.
Sun to shine, rain to fall,

water from a dry well,
a mother's ache relieved.
You are but a beggar

out for a stroll
on this island of brittle bones.
Iguanas bask on granite,

strands of shiny beads swing
on a gumbo limbo tree,
and a blue cotton hospital gown
hangs on the cemetery gate.

Postcard to Elizabeth Bishop
from Key West, 76 Years Too Late

My Dearest—

I stood on your White Street doorstep yesterday, crushed to have
missed you. You won't believe how your little island is changed—
all built up and pell-mell busy, your elegant eyebrow house now a
trendy stop for gawking tourists. I climbed the venerable avocado
tree still holding court in your backyard. I could almost peer
in your bedroom window where you held Louise in your arms,
listened to the June rain patter on the tin roof. Is it rude to say I
wish it had been me? I've never been with another woman, but I
could love you. Last night, I walked down to the fishhouses, and
yes, it is a silver world still, iridescent mahi scales on stone, sea
sequins on metal benches, the water mirrored in the twilight.
Yesterday, I caught a rainbow. Held its colored stripes in my hands.
Watched its ribbons waver with life. Then—for you—I let it go.

Third Time Lucky

Blue is the path I chose, your eyes
lamb-gentle, and I am home

safe as home should be, ought
to be but hasn't been. Until

the day I dove into the sky. Until
breath was unheld, until being

held was like breath, cool whisper
on my cheeks, those neon signs

so used to burning, flashing—
Shame. Rage. Despair.

Until, until, I found the windows,
opened them wide, stuck

my nose out—dog on her first car ride—
leaned my torso into the wind

like a bare-chested beauty
on the prow of a ship. Now.

Blue is the water that sings.
Blue is the water that drowned

the flames. Blue is the color
of redemption. Phoenix rises

into the blue.

Don't Give Up

they call to us from the safety
of their barstools,
where risk-taking consists
of sipping Cuba libres
and arguing over the check.

Don't give up! as Tony and I
salsa the high wire
of the dance floor,
no net, counting our steps,
shuffling and stomping

as if killing fire ants.
It is strange, having lived
in a body for 60 years,
to override its autopilot,
tell it to move in ways

literally foreign.
To unleash hips long held
tight, allow them
to beckon and sway. Like
a mating ritual of two,

rather large, exotic birds.
I'm grateful there are no
mirrors. At the table in front,
a couple smiles, raises
their mojitos. *Don't give up!*

they call as the band switches
to a rhumba. We must look
like giving up is inevitable,
or at least a strong possibility.
But I tell you,

no matter what life plays—
mambo, cha cha, even tango—
there is no "giving up" in us.
On us. We are each one drum
of a double bongo, and the beat goes on.

On her back, her mind wanders

the aisles of Whole Foods
or perhaps the bluffs
of Pierce Stocking Trail.
Such odd appellation—
for both—if one ponders,
and one has the time
each Saturday at ten,
sometimes even Thursday
at four. Surprise!
How lovely lovemaking is
with your very best friend, even
as your brain meanders
and ganders at the cracks
in the ceiling, and Christ,
that light fixture is dusty!
Lust is a funny mixture
of trust and lists. Letting go
and taking stock,
webbing and deflowering,
the sieve and stake of pleasure.
Sheets twisted, damp with sweat,
call the vet, thaw the meat,
cup the balls, pay the bills.
Oh, she's coming! Now she's back
on her back, making love, making lists.

Sonnet While Waiting for the Hurricane

Another woman would have left by now.
Locked, loaded, shot up the artery north
via US 1, back to the safe prow
of the mainland mothership. But of course
I am here on this island, daytime skies
dark with dread. I should be afraid. Instead,
I'm electrified—grown ten times the size
I was yesterday, as though I am fed
by the coming gale. Let me flirt with you,
Ferryman. Row me to the edge of deep.
Let the sea take me until I must choose
between breath and death. We aren't meant to sleep
through a tread-water life. I'll take the waves,
pay the price, bear the pain of being brave.

Cento to My Aging Self

What is this universe
that occupies my face?
The portrait does not reply,
it stares. I lost a lovely smile

somewhere, and many colors
dropped out. What's wrong
with me, Doc? There must be
a pill for this.

Shall I pray? Shall I venerate
and be ceremonious?
The river is rising, approaching
the window in awful nearness.

This is where language will stop,
the horse we have ridden
all our lives rearing up
at the edge of a dizzying cliff.

There will be dying.
There will be dying,
but there is no need
to go into that.

I would say help me
          help me   but listen
I am okay. In the bedroom,
soft skin and old regret

continue their melodious
duet. Even the geraniums
look curious. What if a leaf
could whisper the slow ache

as the green drained away?
Then here I am, the blown peony.
But isn't the air here cool
and wet and almost

unbearably sweet? Isn't it beautiful
when the sun goes down?

Sources:
Ruth Stone (line 1), Elizabeth Bishop (2, 3)
Ocean Vuong (4), Walt Whitman (5)
Wendell Berry (6), Billy Collins (7)
Derek Mahon (8), Alicia Ostriker (9, 10, 13, 15)
Tony Hoagland (11), Ellen Bass (12, 14)

ANN WEIL writes at her home on the corner of Stratford and Avon in Ann Arbor, Michigan, and on a deck boat at Snipe's Point Sandbar off Key West, Florida. Her work has been nominated for Best of the Net and appears in more than 45 journals and anthologies including *Crab Creek Review, Bacopa Literary Review, Whale Road Review, Shooter Literary Magazine, Eastern Iowa Review,* and *DMQ Review.* Ann earned her doctorate at the University of Michigan and is a former special education teacher and professor of education. Read more of Ann's poetry at annweilpoetry.com.

Thank you to my Hot Mess and RedFerns writing groups and to my writing buddies Jackie Craven and Susan Kress for helping me birth and refine these poems. I am also indebted to Morgan Ray and Laura Garfinkel for their most excellent guidance in getting my manuscript in order. Finally, I want to thank my new writing family, Yellow Arrow Publishing, for your mentorship and ongoing support through the publication process. You've made this journey a joyous one.

Thank you for supporting independent publishing.

Yellow Arrow Publishing is a nonprofit supporting writers and artists identifying as women. Visit YellowArrowPublishing.com for information on our publications, workshops, and writing opportunities.